Printed in the USA
CPSIA information can be obtained
at www.ICGtesting.com
CBHW051109081224
18660CB00040B/1353

9 781072 965022